Unseen Instinct: Resilience and the Search for a Why after Murder-Suicide

By J. Amanda

First Edition: September 2021

Unseen Instinct: Resilience and the Search for a Why after Murder-Suicide/ J. Amanda

ISBN: 978-1-943616-49-7

Publisher: MAWMedia Group, LLC

Los Angeles | Reno | Nashville

Dedication

I dedicate this book to my mother. I know she would be proud of me for my achievement and for my commitment to helping others. To my siblings, I offer my love and forever sisterhood. To all who read this, I offer my condolences, my encouragement, and my affirmation.

Table of Contents

Preface

You can survive anything. It is a learning experience from tragedy. The end of trauma is resilience. My mom did not get to live her dreams. I want to present the opportunity for others to see their resilience. I refuse to continue her cycle and keep doing her laundry. My process of understanding my world without my mother is a forced understanding activating an unseen instinct.

Instinct is your first, most primal, processing of the intuition as your brain works to keep you safe. You first want to rule out your responsibility. That is why you look for your fault in the situation whatever it is. Resilience is an unseen instinct. People do not often see their own resilience. They often need to rely on others to tell them what they have seen in them. The instinct of resilience is activated in response to trauma. It is the search for solutions to the mysteries surrounding the trauma. Sometimes the intuition and instinct cause you to blame yourself. The instinct is the automatic reaction to environmental stimuli. Intuition is a learned process. Intuition is the foundation of feelings.

The 5 Ws and the How. This approach creates organization, and it applies to anyone. If you are overthinking or overwhelmed, this is a good place to start. It is a great tool for accessing and engaging your thoughts. It also connects to a skillset that promotes clarity of thoughts and action.

Who is the person. The people involved are critical to understanding motivations, intentions, and actions in the context of personalities. People bring physical form as well as emotional and spiritual elements to their interactions. The motivations are the reasons they create for action. Intentions are what they want as an outcome. Their actions then are the manifestations limited by their capability.

What is a question of things. Anything that is involved in the situation can be a what. It is an all the above: what it is, what it means, what it suggests, and more. In that way what is a first conception of both existential questions and practical reality. What provides pieces of the puzzle but doesn't necessarily provide context.

When a construct of time. Actions are understood in the context of time, but also in the context of sequence. Time order is important to understanding the intentions and reasoning behind what occurs. It reminds me of quality versus quantity in choice behavior. Many people can only function in a clean environment. They wipe counters and wash dishes before they can cook for example. Time order may give some inclination into the origin of behaviors.

Where is about place. The environment of a happening is crucial to understanding the situation and the person. Behaviors are understood in the context of place. A person can be nurtured in an environment or diminished. It reminds me of flight, fight, or freeze choice behavior. Where can cause you stress causing you to either run, battle, or shield yourself. It is the battleground for your thoughts.

Why is everything. It is the reasoning and decision making explained. It is the foundation of the other 5 Ws and it provides insight into the other Ws. Most of use make our decisions influenced by multiple Ws. Yet, in many ways, Why is the key to everything in human behavior. We judge based on the Whys presented when we observe the outcomes of a person's actions.

HOW is figuring out what is going on in the situation. It is the process, steps, and actions in sequence connected to capability. How brings together the 5Ws in an objective view of human behavior. It is

Unseen Instinct

less involved in the emotion and more focused on the dry facts of the matter. It is limited in its concern for the Why. I don't know my mother's Why. I am attempting to confirm mine.

Her Why & My Why

If one of your parents passes, you have lost part of you. When my mom died, a part of me died. I can no longer call her and talk. She is not there for me to argue with for the sake of arguing. Portions of me are off-limits because I don't want to be the person anymore that reminds me of my mother. She is not here anymore, so I am not sure how to navigate the parts of my personality that we shared. My choices do not always resonate with her choices. I don't want to live my life in parallel to hers. Look where she ended up. I don't want to make the choices that put me in the same position.

I read a quote that popped up on my timeline. It was a Winnie the Pooh video. The quote says, "You're braver than you believe, stronger than you seem, and smarter than you think." The quote resonates with everyone. It is a 360-type of quote: bravery, strength, and intelligence. It is communication and resilience.

- **Braver.** I am taking the initiative to write my story. It is not easy telling a story of personal tragedy.

- **Stronger.** I have all the tools to heal. I can do things that you require hard work. I will always have an empty space, and my weakness in that space does not mean weakness in all things.
- **Smarter.** I must use what is available to make the choices in life that matter. I can accomplish things that I never thought were possible.

It was a message from the universe sent especially for me. I don't watch Winnie the Pooh. No one I engage with watches Winnie the Pooh. The video showed up alone from 10 years ago. I saved the quote to pull up later. Next year will be 10 years since my mother passed. I don't know where the recommendation came from, but I am glad it did.

Therapy

Therapy helps you discover your 5 Ws and the H. The Why is the most important for every person. I laugh because the situations, warmup, constructs my therapist presented were general yet engaging and effective. "How are you today?" elicited more information than I could have imagined.

The Why is often missed in therapy. It is difficult to find the Why in this situation. No one can communicate the truth and reasoning that went into the event because it was a murder-suicide. The voices

Unseen Instinct

of those lost are missing from the conversation. That leaves the survivors with questions. There is nothing there in the space where answers are supposed to be. Maybe the Why is in the silence—peace for her. She no longer must go through the abusive cycle she was in. She does not need to continue enduring the lack of love, affection, and belonging that she endured. It is a peace that is not negative or positive. It is neither good nor bad. I don't have peace. I miss her. But I wrestle not wanting to upset her peace in my search for answers. She is resting in peace. Yet I still want to know Why.

Even though I do not know him. I knew her. He did this to her. She did not do this to herself. Knowing the why would not help me. She is gone. What I am looking for is closure. The value in closure is the certain outcome and the answers to your questions. When murder occurs, most have convictions from the court following a process of investigation and a trial. In this case, a murder-suicide, there is no conviction nor punishment. Yet closure is not only conviction and punishment. Blame is not the only outcome.

Reconciliation is the other option. bible verse I know is Romans 8:28. It says, "And we know that all things work together for the good of them that are the called according to His purpose." Many think that this is a restitution quote. It is a reconciliation quote. Reconciliation means that restitution is accessed over time as a work in progress. Reconciliation is not simple. It is a daily choice to keep moving forward. For example, I have my grandmother, but she is not my mother. I can connect with an elder and gain insight from their experience. But my grandmother does not replace my mother. She provides elements of healing that are valuable. Every day when I wake up, my mother is still gone. When she passed, I was living with her. Yet I am choosing to look toward the present and future rather than the past. I am collecting the things that work together for my good wherever I find them.

Resolving My Sense of Self

I recognized a cycle as I grew to college age. She was a young mom with a string of failed relationships. She was cliché in a way—looking for love in all the wrong places. The domestic violence she experienced was brutal. She was once pistol whipped as well as constantly verbally and emotionally abused. As an escape from the unpleasantness of her latest relationship, she found an outlet with a secret person. It was the only way she knew how. She probably did not want to hurt the person she was with, but she had a pattern of easing out of relationships rather than ending them cleanly. She was attempting to figure out her 5Ws and H. She could not figure out a healthier way to get out of the situations she found herself in.

Abuse is painful to every child. It is a constant reminder of powerlessness and vulnerability. Children want to protect their parents especially from an abuser. Yet children cannot protect parents from an unclear, unresolved sense of self. Children cannot provide the

Unseen Instinct

self-esteem, love, and security that is unmet in the hearts and experience of their parents. I could not provide that for my mother. I witnessed the patterns, but I did not know the depths of her needs. I did not know how to provide her with answers. I have accepted through my own work that it was never my responsibility to provide for her.

I am a strong, independent person who does my own laundry. I use the term "laundry" because the analogy is useful. A laundry service includes a certain set of choices. Basic cycles include wash and rinse. You can add fabric softener. You can use specific detergents. Some detergents are more expensive than others. Some clean different from others. You can overload the machine, and nothing gets clean. You can waste money without enough clothes in the machine. The options can be overwhelming to think about.

I am concerned when people connect with people who do not know themselves. They have trouble deciding who they want to be. They have trouble benefitting from the resources that they have around them. They are not dealing with their laundry. They find themselves in the same inferior, deficit-based, unsustainable cycles. My message is to inform their laundry service. Get better detergent. Learn how to sort your colors and delicates. At some point, invest in better laundry equipment, cleaner water, and fabrics that are resilient.

Laundry will always be there until the day you die. You must get better at your laundry as you mature. Your reactions to life must evolve based on the information and opportunities you create. My goal is to provide a foundation for that evolution. This is my WHY.

Unseen Instinct

Section I: The Tragedy

Chapter 1: The Event

I was 21 years old going on 22. It was a week before school started and five days before my birthday. My mother was transitioning from a job without benefits to a job with benefits. It was a difficult transition for her. She was blossoming.

Her father's passing hit her hard. He reached out to her before the end came. "When are you going to come see me?" She did not see him again until he was in a casket. From there, she seemed to find outlet and expression for her aspirations. His passing woke up something of an awareness to her responsibility to her family.

I was always asking her about her ambitions and upward mobility. I wanted more for her before she wanted more for herself. She talked with one of my school counselors to get some information on me. Sneaky! My counselor, to this day, remembers my mother as one of the most comfortable and down-to-earth persons she had encountered in her years of counseling. She also engaged the counselor from some information for herself. She inquired about options, colleges, payments, and opportunities. She wanted to do better for herself. It was simply a motherly instinct. She had plans to go back to school for accounting. She had developed a passion for finance as she realized the opportunities in investments

After her father died, I encouraged her to get life insurance. I was certain that she would not need it for decades. She acquiesced feeling herself within this responsible adulthood experience.

The Last 3 Words

It was morning, my mother came back home from working a live-in shift. She had been gone 2 or 3 days. She looked at her bank account and noticed some overdraft charges. We had some words.

"Jen! You caused me to have charges on my account!" I was upset that she did not remember that I asked her about the need for a workout top. I probably said something that hurt her feelings. I said something very mean. I don't remember what it was, but I know I was angry. I remember saying something that silenced her.

She went to take a shower. After the shower, she got dressed and went out. I knew I had hurt her feelings and attempted to reconnect with her. "Mom, where are you going?"

"I'll be back" was all I heard her say. It was about 2:00pm. I went about my business hanging with a friend at their house. We talked about her business and other things. I am not sure how long I was there, but I do remember noticing a cop car near my house on my way home. I didn't think anything of it beyond the normal questions of why a cop would be on our street. We lived on a busy street. I returned home and focused on my chill mode. It was the week before school. "Where did you Go" by No Mercy was playing as I heard a knock on the door. A detective stood at the door and delivered the news that began tears that flowed the whole night. My mother was never coming home.

I called my extended family members, and many arrived to console me and my siblings. My mother's boyfriend cried. He was hurt as well. He is not my father and did not attempt to console me. He kept to himself. I don't know their relationship other than what I witnessed in my home. I know my mom was not "happy," but I do not know what the specific emotions were. I did not have a relationship with this boyfriend.

I cannot do my mother's laundry. I do not want to find the stains— the damage, emotional pain, and trauma—that she endured. She had twice as many loads to balance I found out later. She was working through something that I will never have complete understanding of. I have surpassed the age that she was when she first had children with no children of my own. I have overcome something of a generational curse. I am living my path without the limitations that my mother held. I hold her in my heart and love her. I feel bad about the missed opportunities to engage, hold, and talk with her. Missed opportunities could be addressed just by visiting your loved ones. Don't miss an opportunity.

The Perpetrator

I did not know the person who took my mother from me. I did not know what their title was. I don't know other details of how they met. I did not know exactly what their relationship was. What I was told through the process was more than I could comprehend. I read the police report and found out much more information than I was ever told.

I did meet him once. I put the clues together to realize that we had Christmas lunch at his place one year. I asked my mother about him as the inquisitive person I was.

"Who is he to you?" She looked down like a child caught in a lie.

"Oh. He's just a friend." Her voice was low. I did not bring it up again. I just let it be.

Her live-in boyfriend did not know that she was nurturing a relationship with another man. I believe her killer was a happy outlet for her. But this was also a pattern for my mother. She would often seek a fresh start with men who were more what she wanted. Each new man was abusive at least verbally. Name calling would begin with assaults on the children. Her feelings hurt; she would defend the children. As an adult, I recognize that she trapped herself as she gave birth to children by these men. I remember one of her boyfriend's calling her children "dead weight." She met the previous boyfriend through online dating. I am not sure how she met her killer.

Her pattern was an endless search for happiness. She engaged with them with a heart full of hopes. When they would show their true colors of abuse, she would respond with moving on—leaving. That may have been the only way she knew how. She was smart and her emotional tools were limited. She knew what she was doing in response to the abusive environment, but she was unable to discern character and a fit with her on the frontend of relationships.

The Whole Story

She had a secret life. I found out that she took off work to meet with him. She was making room for him and this relationship. She got an engagement ring from the guy. She did all this in secret. My mom was attempting to row her boat and it sank. The outlet she was hoping

Unseen Instinct

for became her deathbed. My younger siblings may know more about the specifics, but their grief has rendered them mute. They refuse to speak ill of my mother and her actions. She continues to be their angel, unflawed and perfect in their eyes.

My siblings consider me to be the judgmental one. I am the one who holds them accountable for their choices. I am the sister who holds the standard for the family. I'm the oldest sister. Pressure and responsibility come with that position in the family. I was always opposite from my mother. I lived by my own standards and stood comfortable as an individual. That confidence labeled me as the "stuck up" sister. My siblings have not paid attention to the development and virtue I have grown into. Standards and confidence have graduated into security and vision. I only know how to be me. I can't be the same person I was before. I can't be happy in situations where my standards are disappointed. I desire acceptance as all humans do, but I will not lower myself to obtain it.

I am cautious in relationships. That was the case even before my mother's death. Yet the process of grief, loss, and recovery has helped me mature tremendously. My priority is to elevate myself. I am truly walking along in my life. If I don't like the ship a person is sailing in, I am more concerned about being safe. I apply the tools that I learned in grief counseling. I learned to separate my problems from the problems, experiences, and perspectives of others. Like I said, I will not do my mother's laundry. I will not do other's laundry either. I learned to separate the areas of my life in sustainable compartmentalization. That allowed me to grieve without limiting every other aspect of my life. I don't overload my washing machine loading everything in life at once. I have learned to take time for myself.

Life is short, but you must also realize that you have time. Life is short, but it is not a rush. Many do not apply the tools that are available. They are expressed in the 6 virtues: wisdom, courage, humanity, justice, temperance, and transcendence.

Wisdom is experience, knowledge, and judgment applied to your life as behaviors. It is the foundation of decision making that orders your life in cause and effect.

Courage is strength in the face of fear or the ability to do something that you are not certain you will succeed in. Courage requires that you push through an unknown. As you move forward with perseverance, you find the results whether positive or negative, but you learn regardless of the outcome.

Humanity is our identity within the context of behaviors reserved for human beings. The height is empathy, consideration, and gratitude. The bottom is murder, selfishness, and narcissism. Humanity is what gives rise to emotions. The expression of those emotions reveal character.

Unseen Instinct

Mom is RIP. She was the peacemaker. She did not want us to fight or separate emotionally. Now that she is gone, we have our struggles, but I am confident that we will find our way back together as we find our own identities and our humanity. We also share blood and an experience.

Justice is an expression of your rights, unalienable, human, foundational. Justice includes morality, righteousness, reasoning, and prosocial conduct. It is fairness to yourself and others. It is critical to a civil society because it provides a level playing field, access to resources, and reflectiveness on your impact upon others.

Temperance is application of self-judgement understanding your limits. Extravagant behavior, extreme fluctuations, and overindulgence are opposite qualities. Reasonable, moderate, and measured are synonymous traits. The ability to manage your reactions to the world is critical to your sustainable success including how you benefit and benefit from others.

Transcendence. Your approach, your distractibility, your adaptability, your sensitivity to environment, and your humanity are described in your transcendence. The greater your ability to go beyond the normal or baseline of reaction the greater your transcendence. Transcendence allows you to feel beyond the environment and the circumstance toward a constant sense of gratitude, peace, and inspiration.

Chapter 2: Aftermath

The man my mother was with at the time of her murder she was with felt it was my obligation to tell him something. I did not know anything to tell him. We did not have a relationship. I did not have any information. He was hurt. He felt he should have known. Ten years of relationship and it was over.

He thought I knew because I'm the oldest. He was hurt. But I was not sympathetic. He treated her poorly and us as well. He called us children "dead weight." He didn't understand what having a woman with children entailed. Kids were a tool for keeping relationships. I'm not sure whether it was my mother or the guy, but the reasoning was flawed. It was one step forward, two steps back.

Obligations

My non-existent relationship with her boyfriend was worse after my mom was gone. His childish ways expanded. His demands bordered on making me the replacement for my mom in the home. He expected me to be at his beck and call while cleaning, cooking, and ensuring that my siblings were current on their chores, homework, and hygiene.

My younger siblings were 16 and 12. He didn't understand that the load was too heavy for a 22-year-old. I moved out. I feel regret in some ways. They feel like I abandoned them in some respects. I never called them after leaving. I don't feel guilty. The feeling is that I wish things were different. I wish I was never in that position. I wish my mother was there as she had always been. I was not their guardian. Their father was. My regret was that we could not share out pain and support one another more intentionally. I knew the pain I felt. I knew they felt that pain as well.

My mother's murder and the aftermath continue to be a difficult conversation among my siblings. We don't talk much about my exodus. I cannot give what is expected during the conversations we do have. I am here as a sister. I am a support even as I hold to my standards. I hope that each of my siblings take charge of their lives and make principled choices that move them forward. If not, I will let them know if they are willing to listen. Otherwise, I will nod silently and keep my opinions to myself.

Generational Curses

My mother grew up here and was pregnant at 16 or 18. Young, unmarried, early parents is a trend that runs in my family. Failed relationships run in my family. Some may call it a generational curse. I plan to break the curse. Loving yourself is lost on many in my generation. They want someone from the outside to say it unconditionally. They give birth to children to cope with that desire to be loved in their lives.

My older brother is the first child of our family. The first-born male is the king of the family. He steers the ship. He always knows what he is doing. It's patriarchal. I rebelled against that. My mom wanted American Love in her American Dream. She also wanted the big house, white man, and financial security with all the trimmings.

I was the studious, explorer kid. I wanted to be independent from my older brother. By the time I was in college, I was taking the bus to school—a shock for my mother. Art, dance, and other creative outlets were forbidden by culture. If you want to live higher, she thought, you must spend your time in things that make money. I was told to aim higher. If I did not follow her wishes, I was the reason for her anger.

I'm judged as being analytical and judgmental. They say I'm too hard and that's the reason for their choices. No way! I don't accept that responsibility. They made the choices themselves. That's not my laundry. My mom allowed different standards for my siblings than she had for me. I was left to uphold the standards that I was raised with among my sisters. I argued with mom over her lax attitude and allowances with my sisters. She would get mad and dismiss me. That difference in upbringing amounts to a difference in worldview and perspective on choice and consequences. My hope is not for compliance. I only hope that my sisters accept accountability for their choices.

My Focus Beyond American Love

We never had the birds and bees talk. She once said she would pick someone for me to marry. I proposed that I would choose on my own. I am more focused on the American Dream. American Love can come from anywhere even outside the United States. I'm not following the yellow brick road to a yellow brick house. I'm building my brick house with bricks of any color. I like red. LOL.

My dream is about sharing appropriately the skills I have achieved. I want to care for the less fortunate. I want to assist those who are connecting to help themselves. My goals as a leader includes leadership as an entrepreneur. I want to be free just as my mother did, yet my choices are independent of others. I will achieve my dream without a requirement to leverage others.

Finding a spouse is an option of either dumb luck or compatibility. If he comes, he comes and makes my life better. He shares my values and lives a life of virtue. Guys will hurt you no matter what. If you are not giving them what they want, watch how they act. Always be prepared to walk away. Have the conversations and establish your rules. Commit only when you find the freedom to live your life. His choices must align with yours. Have sustainable fun. That means uplifting, progressive choices that move your dream forward.

I can't say that my mom taught me that, but I can say that being her child has emphasized the importance of prioritizing health, safety, intentionality, and progress over a relationship-dependent concept of love. Find the strength and discipline to focus on your dream first. Do not allow your choices in a moment to limit your future.

Chapter 3: Setup for Healing

I do not use the word healing often, but I do accept that word. I more often discuss it as a process. I don't cry like I used to. I used to ball, cry out my eyes. I still cry, but I shed tears rather than rain tears. I still listen to music from Cambodia even though I do not know the language. I keep them as a reminder of my mother. Though she is not present in those moments, I feel her and find happiness there.

Grief and Recovery

First, recognize that you will need to cry your tears out completely. Allow your emotions to flow freely. Just as I have lessened the number of tears, I have not lessened the emotional energy that is directed toward my loss. The crucial shift for me was to turn that energy toward my progress. Complete the grief stages when they present themselves. Continue to complete them repeatedly if needed.

Unseen Instinct

I had the goal to complete my dreams before I died. I had worked in a mental hospital. I did not want to hurt myself or need medication to function. I want to feel complete in my identity. Even half of them would be an achievement. Nothing less than half. This is important because it is connected to who I am. It doesn't matter how long it takes to achieve it. What matters is the road I take.

Too many don't achieve their spiritual, mental, and emotional goals. They are not comfortable agreeing with their goals. For example, people still go through grief and don't know why. I have particular friends who get stuck in the stages of grief and the stages of development.

Bargaining and Acceptance were the most memorable grief stages for me. I continue to bargain because I am often faced with the reality, I see with others who have their mothers to talk with and interact with. I wish my mother would be back. I don't know the Why of the situation. That is why acceptance is so difficult. I have focused on accepting my personal growth.

I know life is not fair. It will never be fair. Therapy was about putting the pieces back together after the loss and establishing who I am without her here. Most responses to grief are artistic. Like a flower, the growth looks different from the finished bloom. The bloom is what garners the attention and the praise. The growing pains are not often celebrated. The pruning of leaves if not usually something that people talk about.

Recovery is about turning a negative into a positive, turning sadness into happiness, planting a seed into nurturing soil and watching it grow. I have been independent my whole life, but this is another level. I have been independent knowing that my mother was there. I taught myself how to ride the bus, tie my shoes, and more. But now, the experience, the knowledge of my mother being there is gone. She is not here in the physical, but she is here in the spiritual. Whatever role she is in, she is there. I know she is. Knowing that she is looking over me gives me comfort.

A medium told me that my mother drops coins on the ground—literal money—to show that she has been where I am. I call them tokens because they are symbols of an emotional feeling. The image encourages me. Each time I see a coin, I am awakened to a greater awareness of my environment. It reminds me of the old saying, "Leave a token of gratitude." She leaves these manifestations of her caring for me to find in my daily life. They are reminders of her.

Loss Learning

Self-acceptance is the greatest thing I learned. Accepting myself as resilient is an identity question that must be answered. People must become more aware of how they feel and how they see things. The need is for awareness of your inner being. Your greatest power is your power of choice. You have your own path that you create with each choice you make.

Find what makes you happy. Do what makes you happy. Examine the results of your choices and determine if the happiness gained is the happiness you desire. Happiness is living the life that you desire every day. This is what we strive for. But happiness is more about feeling the autonomy to make the choices rather than the results themselves. People are only accessories to your happiness.

People say that they can never be happy, but that is confirmed because of what they say. When you speak sadness, that is the result. It is your option to turn that energy into something different. All the emotion is energy. Leaves turn for a reason. They indicate the seasons. The seasons in your life will continue to change.

Emotional Acceptance

What you experience is yours to determine. Happiness or something different is ties to your perspective. That is why your emotional support is so critical. With that emotional support, you can gain emotional acceptance.

Emotional acceptance is the ability to allow whatever is going on in the moment. The trigger is present that causes you to feel something. Being mindful of your emotion in the moment is critical to your emotion management. I am not the expert in this, but I know the process. Triggers come from multiple directions. It can be a song, a date, hormones, or people.

Two elements that I researched and support my emotional acceptance are autonomy and self-efficacy. Autonomy has confirmed that it is my role and responsibility to do what I want in my life. I am the decision maker. I make the world I want to see. Self-efficacy is the ability to act in the spaces I find myself and to create additional spaces through my interactions—spaces to act in my best self-interest.

My good friends share their grief stories. One has a mother who passed due to ALS. Another has a father who died. Most of my friendships are with people who know grief in a personal way. I met them in different stages of their grief compared to mine. My friend whose father died always talks about him. She keeps his memory alive by talking about the great person he was. I resonate with the emotions felt in their stories. The same reactions, steps—the process of grief— are common to everyone. They don't always occur in a certain order, but they are always present.

That shared experience gives me comfort even though they do not necessarily know the whole story. My emotional acceptance allows me to determine whether friends are friends for a season or friends for a reason? I have another friend who has turned his grief into a blessing for others, but his speech is often negative. The emotions he faces are his alone, but negative emotions bring you down. Always.

Unseen Instinct

Count your blessings is what some would say, but I am not counting. I am focusing each day on adding one more blessing to my life. It is not an accounting, but an active engagement with my world utilizing my choices to my benefit and the benefit of those around me. That is what my friend does. He rents his mother's former home out to people who need a place to say. That is turning a negative into a positive. That is living a life beyond grief making the most out of a bad situation.

Section II: The Process of Healing

Chapter 4: Getting over the Hill

My mom never went to college. She made the decision to have kids early on. Her focus was raising children. I trust that she decided to have a family in lieu of other options that were just as possible for her. I fear that motherhood was a means to obtain and maintain love. That is a feature that seems present in our family history. I don't think she truly had other options presented to her. A professional career was not a dream for her. She updated her dreams as she got older, but she didn't have a chance to fully pursue them.

I am choosing another path. Kids, I know, are an expense that I am not ready for. I want them later, but now, the work and effort of relationship building, birthing, and childrearing does not fit for me or my life. I know child rearing is a career in itself. I want another career first.

Moving beyond, refusing, solving a generational curse may be the most difficult of propositions because it seems that you are powerless in a self-fulfilling prophecy. That is true when you attempt to address the demons and ghosts of your ancestors all at once. It is less true when you approach your individual life one decision at a time. Rather than being overwhelmed with the task, you learn, grow, and make the best choice each time you are faced with a decision. Your learning guards against fallacies and ignorance that others may have been limited by. Your growth secures you against choices made due to low self-esteem, insecurity, or feelings of obligation. Your best choice will then rise from the power to select or create from an increased set of options.

Finishing School

My mom wanted better for her kids. She did not say it out loud, but she pushed us in her own way. I think all parents want better for their kids. Yet those kids make the final decisions. Parents are ultimately not responsible for the choices their children make. But that does not let them off the hook. They are responsible for the environment and the decision-making skills that their children grow up with. Use of reinforcement, psychology, and influence combine with example to train kids in the ways they should go.

My mom was not quiet, but many things related to reinforcement, psychology, and influence were left unsaid. She never voiced that she was proud of me, but she would always tell other people about my accomplishments. She would play Usher's "You Got

Unseen Instinct

it Bad" and miss my oldest brother who was in the navy. That was her way of showing love for him though she wasn't consistent at saying it face-to-face. She was talkative but did not have the courage to say it out loud. She would celebrate milestones but was hesitant to offer praise.

Our relationship was about a silent communication of love, support, and pride. Each of my siblings can recount their own specific way she engaged with them. I remember finishing my driving test and her insistence that we go to Red Lobster. Not a word about the achievement. The waiter at Red Lobster could have concluded that nothing special had happened. We only wanted food. But I knew that the impromptu lunch date was her way of communicating her pride in my accomplishment.

My mom didn't finish college, so I want to accomplish that for myself and her. It's more survival for me than it is doing it for her. But I honor her in my achievements. Nursing is rewarding for me. People who are less fortunate or unable to care for themselves are helped by nurses. I feel appreciated working in that field. My natural ability to help people drew me to this profession. The fact that my mom would be proud is a bonus inspiration rather than a motivation.

Letting Go of the Dream

If my mom was here, I would have reached farther quicker in life. I must take it slowly and that is okay. The loss is not primarily about timing. It is about an emotional foundation that allows me to take risks, bounce ideas, and know that my navigation is supported. Living at home, idle conversation, and an environment of support would make a difference in my pace and position in life. Knowing that you have someone who believes in you propels you to move beyond your strength and push forward. You want to accomplish things before birthdays, anniversaries, or ages. You are motivated to bring that degree or achieve that raise so that mom will be proud. That's the way it could have been.

I was forced to be on my own without my mom. That is the reality I operate within each day. Your support system makes all the difference. The fear of the unknown increases as you face a loss. You never know how dark the world is until you lose someone. The process of loss, especially when you lose someone who you count on, requires new sources of support. It's okay to cry in those supportive environments. That expression of emotion is a step in the direction of healing. Sharing that emotion is a step toward relationships that help you through the roughest of times.

Everyone is different when it comes to grief. I was in a funky age when my mom died. I had to keep floating when she passed. I was at an age of being unsure. I was at an age where I assumed that my

Unseen Instinct

mother could bear some of the weight of my fluctuating emotions and flighty decision making. I knew I could lean on my mother for financial, emotional, and physical support when needed. After she was gone, I had to come to terms with the fact that I would not have my mother to help me through it. The assumptions I had leaned upon were suddenly gone. I had to grow up quickly and stand on my own.

I resolved above all to be positive. Coping with the loss is about positivity. I set about cultivating positivity through reading. Luckily, I was able to take Psychology courses and learn about grief and loss as well as self-efficacy and more. The 5 elements of self are critical in loss and all areas of life. They are as follows:

- Self-awareness.

- Social skills.

- Motivation.

- Self-regulation.

- Empathy.

These elements become intertwined during a loss and must be unraveled. Just as you learned to crawl, walk, and run, you must learn how to cope, endure, and grow. Each person must decide for themselves what their coping, endurance, and growth looks like. Everyone adopts their own role after a loss like this. I remember my attempts at stepping into a coordinator role for my siblings. I found that they were not ready for that. They are afraid of being judged. That's common to all people. No one appreciates being judged.

When my mom was alive, we shared and competed motivating each other to think big. Something of a foundation, trust, and comfort was lost when mom was gone. Everything has gone silent. As quiet as my mother was, her children communicated while she was alive. It changed with her passing. We no longer seem to connect. I still reach out as I can connect. The results are hit and miss.

The Puzzle

School became an information store for figuring out the 5-Ws and the How. I was a puzzle that needed to be reconnected in the context of a self that needed to be unraveled. I was a box of Christmas lights with no chance of throwing them away and starting over. The painstaking process of disentangling had to be completed even while I was attempting to reconnect me as a whole without my mom and without the familiar interactions of my siblings.

I found the space to do that unraveling and reconnecting in therapy. More than grief counseling, therapy can help you better yourself. I attended a grief support group. That was great for community, but the individual work was vital. That work was done during therapy sessions with a therapist that listened. I found that I

Unseen Instinct

was able to pull from my past, make connections to the present, and map out a positive future in that therapy room.

The critical ability is decision making. Self-awareness is the primary skill in the decision-making ability. Know who you are or find out. Try new things and judge whether they fit your desires, morals, and experience. Build character as your primary concern.

Communication is the second required skill. Holding in your feelings can stifle you and constipate you emotionally and physically. That constipation results in illness both emotionally and physically. Build your social skills including refusing to share when sharing is inappropriate.

Consistency is the next skill. You must engage the counselors and other supports repeatedly to gain results. Checking in secures your perspective on life and the options available to you. Build intrinsic motivation that is not dependent upon circumstance, mood, or other outside influences.

Resource procurement is the next skill. You must know how to continue your development and practice. The information you need for mental Heath is at your fingertips with the Internet. Mental Heath resources and days off are available for workers these days.

Empathy is the final skill. Cultivate the ability to see events from their perspective and to trace the steps of their decision making. I know that my mom was not happy or satisfied. I know that she was searching for that happiness. She was just beginning to realize that happiness does not require a relationship with a man. She was learning to make the dream her priority. I recognize that and am able to heal as I disentangle my disappointment and sense of loss from my anger at the person who prematurely ended her development.

Several types of therapy exist. You may need one type or multiple types. The point is to gain perspective. From there, you can build your environment of happiness. The goal is to live a life of acceptance. Accept life for what it is even while making the best choices for You. Bad things are going to happen. You don't need to agree or disagree. Release yourself from needing to control the situations. Identify the 5Ws and the How, influence what you can, and accept what you cannot change.

Chapter 5: Sharing Appropriately

It is hard to figure out how much to share. I began by telling people all the 5Ws when they would ask me, "What happened to your mother?" I have determined to answer the question in the simplest of terms.

"She died." Most people will automatically ask the next logical question.

"Oh no. What happened to her?" If I respond with the fact that she was murdered, they want to know more. They are curious about the events. I think people naturally seek comparisons. They want to judge their lives by the lives of others. That type of interest does not serve me well. Once I was older and less tangled with my scenario. I limited my answer to limit the personal reminder and trigger myself to miss my mother.

People do not think about the trauma revisited upon a person each time they tell a story of trauma. It is up to each person to deal with their trauma at their own pace. I am not the same person that I was when my mother died. I did not realize the levels of needing her until later in life. The loss is not just a moment in time that a person can say, "That was a long time ago." My mother is not alive to help, witness, or support me through significant points in my life. Each milestone and achievement cause me to relive the loss in new ways. The loss becomes fresh grief at a moment's notice.

My Experience

You don't control anything but your choices. You get to choose the life you want. You get to choose your 5Ws and your How. In adulthood, you can recognize that the trauma is real, but the recovery is real as well. Your path of comfort and resilience may not be the same as someone else. It will be incomplete if you have lost a parent. Yet, the determination of your success is yours independent of what others think.

We often take on the responsibility to worry about the choices of others. You may be able to influence their decision making prior to choices, but it makes no sense to be angry and thrown off after the decision is made. You may get caught up seeing disappointment as a situation that makes you stuck. You may think that you only have one option being painted into a corner. But...NO.

No one has the vision you have. That cuts both ways. You can't control through your vision. You also are unable to shape their vision

Unseen Instinct

through anger and worry. Sharing, support, and communication is the process. That engagement can change the world.

Sharing. I know that my experience is important to share. The story is touching to illustrate how you can continue a path even through grief. The key ingredient is courage. The memory creates triggers that may doom your progress and your motivation to engage with the world. You may find it hard to live in your truth. Any resistance stifles your creativity of emotions. You get stuck in simple terms. Your emotions are tangled up and may only express as anger, disappointment, and revelry. Anger is insidious when you're immature. Maturity propels you into a greater empathy for others and their choices.

Seek therapy that is more than going to a doctor to begin the process of disentangling. Spend time in nature. Enjoy good music. Travel to places you have never seen. Have experiences that you have never had. Many people don't realize the opportunity to do those things sustainably. They may find nature without balance, music that creates drama, travel that is out of budget, and experiences that include drugs and alcohol. You can do what you want, AND you can make it count and support progress in your life.

Support. I support through my drive and resilience. Coping can be temporarily obtained through substances and unsustainable choices, but coping can also be obtained through seeking help and an environment of healing. Adjustment to your new reality, establishment of your truth comes from the choices that you make. Resist the inclination to use the loss as a crutch and reason for your unsustainable choices.

Another way to think of it is that your support of others inspires them to heal. As Marianne Williamson is quoted:

> As we let our light shine, we unconsciously give other people permission to do the same. As we are liberated from our own fear, our presence actually liberates others.

My greatest support was within myself. I had to conquer my own battles myself. I sought help, information, and perspective, but I had to do the work and put all that assistance together. I had to muster the perseverance. I mustered the audacity to believe that healing was possible for me. I accessed the patience to take my healing day by day.

Communication. The communication makes all the difference. I found that my communication was best completed through writing. Sharing aloud is still difficult for me. Healing can be signaled by an ability to communicate the story, but you are not required to expose yourself to the world. I choose not to make the story about me. I keep my appearance secret. I refuse to be judged by my appearance, how I live my life, and the visible aspects of my person. I choose to keep the story at the center and the healing at the center of that story. I communicate the message. I want the message to speak for itself.

There will be times that you must battle yourself. You must take this road alone even after engaging with those who have helped. You are at war with yourself and your emotions. You can access and communicate your truth. You will feel a power as you are able to live within your truth. Greater than the power, you will find peace.

Appropriate Empathy

I work in the medical field. I most often give through work and volunteering rather than speaking and sharing. Empathy comes naturally to me. I have realized my skill and heart that is caring for others. I recognize where people need assistance, the resistance they must overcome in seeking it, and the other barriers they face. I recognize that the therapy, assistance, or guidance I provide is not the solution. The solution is only found within the person. They are on their own with the final decisions of healing, but I provide the compassion and supportive environment for that decision to be made. I remind them through encouragement and empowerment to make that decision repeatedly.

I must also work to ensure that I do not experience compassion fatigue. Therefore, the provision of empathy and compassion requires that I take care of myself. I need a mental health break from time to time. I must give myself the same care as maintenance as I present to others as healing.

Sharing includes sharing with me. You must take a break from the hard work you are doing to carry the heavy load. You can do your laundry every day. You will be overwhelmed. You will go crazy always sorting and washing. You will get dizzy in the spin cycle if it never stops. You find yourself all wet if you never find some time to relax in the sun. You will be burned out if your dryer is always going.

Trust Issues

I have been challenged to trust people. Trust is a connection including a why related to another person. I was always a trusting person as a child. Trauma after trauma has taught me to apply more caution and discernment rather than trust. The more you observe human nature, you become aware of the motivations, intentions, and aspirations of others. People do not always have your best interest at heart. When the choice between their benefit and your benefit presents itself, most will choose themselves before they choose you.

For me, a great failure that challenge my ability to trust resulted from my intentional sharing of my personal story. I stopped doing that

Unseen Instinct

because those people shared my story. The result was people coming to me, asking questions, and seemingly gaining some fascination without recognizing the private, painful, challenging reality I was experiencing.

Another situation caused me trauma and social life because of a bad investment deal. When you are young, you tend to trust other people. This person had credible communication. His story was like mine. He was a college graduate and seemed wise. He provided me the information on flipping homes.

The scam was based on using my investment to invest in homes. I gave him $50,000 of my inheritance money to engage in the business. I won a civil case by default. I had to pursue him at the state level him as well. I learned to do my homework before trusting. The more lucrative financially or emotionally, the more research and verification is required.

I approach relationships with caution now. Shared stories and similarities are easier to research. If a person is beyond my understanding, if they have different skills and information, I hold them at arm's length until I understand their context, motivations, and morals. I also recognize how to engage with "friends for a reason" and "friends for a season."

Some people are friends for a reason. They are long-term connections because of what they provide for you and what you provide for them. Healthy friendships for a reason are reciprocal. Both parties give and take.

Friends for a season are short-term, but still based on the reciprocal exchange. Without the reciprocal exchange, you are not talking about friendship. You are only speaking of acquaintances. Sharing in those situations is tenuous at best. Telling people about what you have, what you have been through, and providing information about your family and details about your person is dangerous. People can take advantage of you when they know too much about you. You will have trouble knowing them when they can disguise themselves due to what they know about you.

Karma is the law that you cannot run from. The fool that scammed me died. His prison is the grave.

Chapter 6: Adulthood and Identity

I was 16% of the pie in my life. The first four were great. Another two were added. I was born in Long Beach, California. We moved to the Bay Area for a culture shock. It was a different environment and a different language. In LA, "hecka" and "hella" were not words. I also had to wear a uniform in school. My siblings seemed to conform to the environment. It was easy for me because we moved in the Summer months. The ease expired over time.

The disconnect is felt because the glue is not present. We talked everyday as children in the home. Even my brother in the Navy would call most every night. The shattering of our family resulted in cracks even for the children my mother left behind. We are casually acquainted, but the engagement is not what it used to be. I miss talking, laughing, and giggling about everything. Adulthood comes with some changes, but our transition was much more of a split than a healthy growth and change in relationship.

Esther Profile

1990, I was the second of the first batch of 4 kids. My father was a state trooper at the time. I don't know much about him, but that is what I heard. My mom went on to another boyfriend in 1996. She had two other children with him. In 2000, my youngest sibling was born. It was 2004 when my mother met a boyfriend that would move her to the Bay Area. It was the summer after my 9th grade year.

I never liked my mom's boyfriends. Neither of them treat her well. They did not treat us well either. I watched her endure treatment that I did not appreciate. As a child, I wanted to see my mother loved and respected. I wanted her to be shown gratitude. I wanted more good than bad. Every person should be appreciated. Yet my mother always had a type. She liked kinetic men who mostly worked with their hands and drank as a pastime.

I always saw my mom as an Esther character from the Bible. She was beautiful and a dutiful wife candidate. She would cook, clean, and provide a stable household. Yet she never found the king that would respect her. She treated them like kings, but they were never regal. She found the Bay Area boyfriend online on a dating website. She was bored and it was showing in her demeanor and mood.

Developing Adulthood

The challenge is to recognize the social and emotional relationship that is appropriate as we age without the examples of mother. Just the emotional presence of my mother is what I miss most. I am left to discover myself sorting through shattered pieces of a life I once shared with my mother.

Adulthood is about becoming who you are. You determine what you want to do and what you do not want to do. It is a process of self-discovery. Some give up on one thing and pursue others with vigor. Before my mother passed, I did not want to depend on her. I learned to take the bus. I did not want to deal with what was going on at home. I taught myself to get a job. School was a place that I could focus. The noise of home was deafening. School offered a different type of noise—much more productive.

My first career choice was that of a teacher. Honestly, I was so young that the money was the only thing that appealed to me about the profession. As I got older, I developed a sense of the good that teachers could do. I wanted to make a difference in the lives of others. I also relished the creativity that was evident in schools. Every teacher had their own style and my child-eyes perceived this as celebrated and powerful.

In junior high school, I was exposed to various fields. I spent time as a para-educator. It was enjoyable, but something was missing. I enjoyed working with disabled children more than working with the mainstream kids. The experience was more rewarding. I could provide a level of care that was vital and appreciated.

Medical practice appealed to me. I dabbled with med technology, medical stenography, and other tech positions. Caregiving is what my mother did before she passed. I found that caring for people fit me. It felt natural—like where I needed to be. I progressed from caregiver to Certified Nursing Assistant (CNA) to a program for Licensed Practical Nurse (LVN).

The best part of my work is to provide the assistance that people need. Handicaps are more diverse than physical. Everyone needs assistance in some form. That is adulthood. But it is also the life cycle. The sharing of time and energy to encourage friends, educate children, build ramps, counsel people, and more enrich the how, who, what, where, and why of life.

Identity in Life

Life offers many options for becoming in the face of trauma. Grief assistance and counseling offers a chance for healing, but it is not always accepted with varying results. My siblings had varying results from counseling or their refusal of counseling. I think my oldest brother experienced the loss the worst. Other siblings may be fearful of revisiting the trauma. I do not know what their barrier is specifically. I only know that counseling helped me. First, I was able to talk about

Unseen Instinct

what happened. From that starting point, not always focused on what happened to my mom, I was able to talk about what I wanted to happen to me. My 5 Ws and the H were explored. I was able to express myself.

Counseling provided a safe space for me to pick up the shattered pieces. I did not know who I was after my mom passed. In the process, I did not discover anything new about myself at the time. That person was overwhelmed. The past was broken. I had to continue forward without my mother. I used the help to figure out the puzzle of me utilizing some of the broken pieces.

I taught my siblings to tie their shoes. I also taught myself. I created a loop with each string and tied them together. It was not the traditional way to tie shoelaces, but it worked for me. That difference or creativity is something that I have never forgotten though I now tie my shoes the traditional way. No matter whether you go to Harvard or Cal Poly, you will receive a degree at the end of your education. No matter your story, the goal in my mind is to make a difference.

Each person has their own story. No matter how you tie your life together, the outcome is what you make it. Take your time. Listen to your heart. Hear the advice from others. Get help from professionals. Make your decisions based on the reality you want to see. Life is not always the same for you as it is for others. Accept that you are different and have a different story to live out. You also have a different story to write.

Life is my structural program. I have routines that are not always followed, but the point is to include value, joy, and even variety in your life. I remember as a para-educator that the school was structured to provide what was called "centers." Centers are different structured experiences to teach certain subjects to the kids. The brilliance of the experience is to create more individualized engagement even in a larger class of students. This can be an approach to structuring your life. It is a metaphor for exploring different options before you settle. You can also experience multiple experiences through the weeks and months of your life. The variety supports creativity and options. Options support resilience and your continuing progress no matter what trauma you face.

Section III: Resilience and Recovery

Chapter 7: Written in Stone

When loss occurs in your life, you naturally seek answers. So many have felt the same way you feel. I remember hearing someone say, "The experiences of life, good or bad, require you to live through your purpose. There is no higher calling." If I had offspring, I would be able to tell the story in a way that honors my mother, my siblings, and my experience. This book is natural way for me to crystalize my process and communicate what I have learned to date.

Honoring Life and Loss

I write this to honor my mother and the life that she has inspired me to live. The greatest honor, I feel, is the communication of the message my mother left behind. Like much of her communication, it was not something that she said aloud. It was the Why that blossomed within me because of my grief. Create your happiness alone before attempting to find someone to create it for you. Get professional help

Unseen Instinct

if you have trouble. Amateurs, quasi-professionals, and part-time lovers will only muddy the waters and poison the well.

I know for a fact that there is a person for you to talk to whatever you face. You may be in search of your 5Ws or another challenge to your perspective. You can get unstuck when you are stuck. You have multiple avenues when you face challenges. You alone stand with the challenge, but you can gain tools and perspective with help from others who have been trained to walk you through uncertain pathways.

You attend school to gain information about the world, languages, physics, and nature. You learn until the day you die. The way you carry yourself, live up to your expectations, or apply your morals is supported by the information you have learned. People are another influence. You will always have influence from others. Your family is the foundation of that influence. Never be too smart to learn. Never be too embarrassed to be corrected. Never be too afraid to try.

I grew up and explored along the way. I continue to explore to this day. My influence is as important as the influences that have impacted me. Be aware of all the influences that engage you. Continue to explore and make the choices today to impact your tomorrow. Stay awake. That awareness begins with knowing yourself, investigating the influences of family and experience, and committing to creating your own happiness.

Compassionate Caring

My work comes naturally for me. As a caregiver, I can communicate my compassion and share in another person's healing. I consider compassion to be a genetic trait passed down from my mother. Chronic disease requires a steady response and patience with patients who may be frustrated with the recurrent difficulties they face. Acute situations require focus, intention, and calm in the face of time constraints and other's frustrations. The person I am becoming seeks mastery of both.

I am not interested in being a motivational speaker, but I watch them for inspiration and energy. I also listen to TD Jakes and others. I do want to be a registered nurse and live comfortably. I want to work 3 days a week and enjoy my life the other 4 days of the week. I aspire to earn $150,000 per year and more though I do not limit myself. I expect to expand beyond those numbers, but the point for me is to live a happy life.

"Never early. Never late. I've lived enough life to see the potential that started a miracle."

The question of How to be happy is crucial in life. Though I lost my mother at a young age, I still must find the roots of happiness within myself. The roots are at the foundation of your soul. The mind, body, and soul have their own separate roots. You must return to the origin—where you come from. Steve Harvey, a motivational speaker, told me to go back to my roots. He used the imagery of a farmer to model life. You are a farmer cultivating yourself as a plant. Continue to nurture, water, and develop yourself. Take care of you first. You need to be healthy to take care of others.

Better Alternatives

The goal is a better life for everyone impacted. Understanding makes two words with import when you break them down. You are still under when you are standing. Standing in your truth and awareness while still being under—an acceptance of your position and posture learning from the 5 Ws and How.

Refuse to allow others bring you down and limit your potential. Don't wait on other people to do what you want to do. Do what you must to get where you want to go. Connect with people who want to move forward and are moving forward.

How do you make certain that you make an impact on the world? I don't know the answer for you. You must make that determination for yourself. I can influence your foundation, your morals, your sensitivities, and passions, but you must accept, develop, and activate on your own. I can hold the door open for you but must move through it or create your own door or window.

In physics, momentum is created when there is a force present providing a push to potential energy. Inertia is the tendency of an object to stay still. Friction can limit. You are the same. Accept the push from whatever source. Refuse the inertia. Limit the friction. Continue with the energy derived from sustainable sources to continue the push through tough times and the temptation to stop. Rest when you need to but keep moving forward consistently even if your progress is slow.

My morals include self-respect, self-love, authenticity even in your emotions, patience, mindfulness, and a sense of humor. I do not always express my sadness. I convert it to joy from the inside out. I am continually processing emotions. Sometimes, it can seem that I am hiding, but I am intentional to only share what is useful in situations. This is a critical way to express self-love. I share with people in situations where I am certain to receive the support to process and handle the emotional energy. Otherwise, I turn negative situations into positives by using my creativity to create satire, parody, or another funny situation.

Overthinking is the death of emotions on the inside. Mindfulness is processing and feeling along with engaging systematically. That often means serenity—challenging the things that you can change and accepting the things that you cannot change. Knowing the difference, as the saying says, is the greatest gift.

Chapter 8: Overcoming Tragedy

The challenge in thinking and talking about the tragedy is that my mother will never come back. I share when the story can help someone else, but it is true heartbreak that I do not want to relive. Losing a boyfriend can be a heartbreak, but it is nothing compared to the deep connection you have with a parent. Losing a parent brings up emotions you do not know you have. Your love for your parent is mysterious in a way. The fear of loss is more intense when you have lost a parent. My situation is also that my father is not present in the most significant way. That means that I am faced with two losses in different ways in my life. They are different parts of myself that I do not have. The puzzle that is me will never be complete.

Coping

You must face the need for help and work to utilize the help in the way that you perceive it. The hardest thing for me is that the journey that is a walk with my mother has reached an end. I wished things for her that she wanted to accomplish. She had dreams. She wanted a better life. She wanted a better life for me. She cannot continue along that path, but I will.

Coping is the beginning step in grief work. Adaptation is the advanced step. Counseling was a large part of my coping. I don't attend every day now, but I made more frequent sessions in the beginning. Times change. Also, my life cannot completely be about grief and loss.

Awareness. In my coping, I have become aware of my situation. I have leveraged that awareness to adapt to a life without her. I had to determine what healthy steps I must take to keep myself safe.

Acceptance. I must accept the battles that I will face alone most of the time. I must accept and seek out the assistance when it is available. I must cultivate and practice techniques to address the world and interact.

Unseen Instinct

Adaptation. I would cry all the time in the early days. I have come to a point where I am all cried out. The feeling lingers, but it does not create the waterfall that it once was. Reminiscing can be tough. I have moments when I think about the grandmother she would have been and the daughter I would grow to be. I allow myself to cry when I feel those moments.

I am more understanding and patient with people. I am measured when engaging with situations even when I am wronged. I remember a repo company that characterized me as harassing when I had never harassed. I sued them for my personal belongings, and they expected that I would be combative and inappropriate. They prepared for that reality. I showed up and conducted myself as I have adapted.

I learned to manage my anger after losing my mother. I remember getting angry with her about things when she was alive. I wasted too much time with arguments and feeling some way. Life is too short. Loss occurs in a moment. I adapted to life without her.

Identity

Coming to terms with what you have experienced and accepting it in an integrated way is critical. People tell me that I am strong and independent and provide great advice. I am observant and insightful when evaluating people and discerning their character and feelings.

I am patient and help people with their anxiety. People have good intentions, but we do not know the outcomes. You don't know the end result. That provides a level of freedom from worry and regret. Know what you are doing. Do it intentionally.

Many people get frustrated because they don't know the end result. Often, people get stuck or they don't get the results they hoped for in a situation. This causes them to lose patience with situations when they take longer or have more steps than desired. I am often able to help in those situations. I have a great deal of patience to share. I learned that in medicine and through my approach to communicating and listening. I have practiced comprehending people and their choices, providing them with the benefit of the doubt and time to explain.

My mother provided a great example of patience having 6 children. That many children would drive you crazy if you are not patient. They are always around you with traffic. They are always with you. The experience can be overwhelming.

Your Best

Determine where you are and commit to building. Your best self has at least 5 elements in my experience: Recovery, Acceptance, Help-Seeking, and Listening.

Unseen Instinct

Recovery is ongoing. I will never have the puzzle completed. I will never know the complete Why of the event. The road does not promise to lead anywhere. It is quiet, silent with space for coping and adaptation. It leads to more questions about myself and my own Why. Maybe it is a Why to teach new possibilities to others. The search for answers can help me and help others. Emotional support system is the first critical element of recovery. This is the foundation of your recovery. Identify the people in your circle who can provide whatever they can provide. They do not need to offer all the answers.

Acceptance. The critical element to living your best is accepting the variety in people. With that, you accept that every person will not and is not required to like you. You are not required to lose yourself or make yourself small to accommodate anyone. Above all, accept that happiness comes from the inside out.

Help-Seeking avenues for help are also crucial. Many people do not feel that they need help and refuse to seek it. They don't see that the situation is difficult enough to need help. They guess that they already know what the persons will say. They think they already know the answers or should know the answers. Help seeking doesn't always result in help. The key is to understand the help needed, the professionals available, and the fit between helper and you. Recovery is possible when you get the help you need with the fit that works for you.

Listening. Seek additional help from your spiritual being. The critical activity is to get beyond yourself. Understand that you are not the only person feeling this loss. You are not the only one responsible for unfair requirements. Also know that you can heal, and healing is bigger than you. Your identity is not that of victim or survivor. You are You. Take a look at You from the outside in. A spiritual perspective can help with that view of yourself.

www.ingramcontent.com/pod-product-compliance
Lightning Source LLC
Chambersburg PA
CBHW050606280326
41933CB00011B/2000